INTRODUCTION

For many years I have driven past the Alabama Hills c[...] that they possess some significance. Then, on a trip to Death Valley, high winds forced us to camp at Diaz Lake, just on the outskirts of Lone Pine, California. To kill time, we visited the Lone Pine Film History Museum (www.lonepinefilmhistorymuseum.org) and learned about all the movies that have been filmed in the Alabama Hills.

On a subsequent trip, we planned to spend a couple of days in the area and visit the film locations using the Movie Road Self-Guided Tour booklet that is available at the museum. While gathering information on the internet for our trip, I learned about the arches that are found in the Alabama Hills, and we decided to spend some time searching these out, as well.

Eugene Carsey's website (http://www.eugenecarsey.com/camp/Alabama hills /arches2.htm) has a wealth of information on the arches and another good source is Bob's Arches (http://users.sisna.com/archman/AlabamaHills.html). The information on these two sites was helpful in locating arches, but what I felt was needed was a hardcopy that could be used in the field. After discovering that no such resource existed, I began this project of assembling data in the form of a guide booklet that can be used on location. All of the pictures, GPS coordinates, and descriptions in this guide originate from my explorations in the area.

"What is the attraction of searching out natural arches?" you may ask. Well, let me attempt to answer that question. For some, it is simply seeing the interesting forms created by natural processes. For others, it is the photographic opportunities. Many of the arches create stunning views that change continuously with the position of the sun and weather conditions. Being at the right place at the right time can produce profound, surreal, and inspirational photos. For some people it's the thrill of discovery, kind of like an Easter egg hunt. It could also be a reason to get outdoors to camp, hike, and be with family. And in this technological age that we live in, it could be just the rewarding challenge of successfully navigating with a GPS. For me, it was all of the above.

My hope is that when people learn of the arches here, and want to visit them, that my guidebook will provide them with an easy means of accomplishing that task. There is one caveat, however, and that is that this endeavor can get in your blood and you will be hooked.

HISTORY

The Alabama Hills were named by local miners sympathetic to the Confederate cause during the Civil War. They were honoring the CSS Alabama, a propeller driven sloop-of-war that burned or captured 65 Union ships before being sunk by the USS Kearsarge in 1864.

Since the early 1920s, the Alabama Hills have been used as a location for filming movies and television programs. Some recent movies filmed here include Iron Man and Transformers: Revenge of the Fallen.

In 1969, the BLM designated the Alabama Hills as an official Recreation Area. It has become a travel destination for people who like to camp, fish, off road motor tour, mountain bike, ride horses, rock climb, hike, explore movie locations, and take pictures.

GEOLOGY

The Alabama Hills are visually different than the Sierra Nevada mountains, but they are actually both part of the same mountain building process (orogeny). The rock is composed of greatly weathered granite. It is a difference in weathering and erosion that gives the Alabama Hills a unique appearance compared to that of the Sierras to the west. The granite of the Alabamas has been subjected to chemical weathering during its burial in sediment that caused iron in the rock to oxidize giving it an orange tint (iron oxide). In addition, the lower elevation of the Alabamas, when compared to the Sierras, means they are exposed to less snow and ice during the year but more erosion by wind, blowing sand, and water. The rock of the Alabamas is very jointed and broken due to expansion as the weight of overlaying rock was removed during uplift. It is the combined processes of erosion and weathering along these joints that created the arches of the Alabama Hills.

CAMPING

There are several camping options available in and around the Alabama Hills. One option is to camp for free (boon docking) in the Alabama Hills Recreation Area. This is BLM land and dispersed camping is allowed for 14 days. Another option is to stay at one of the area's developed campgrounds. These include Tuttle Creek, Portagee Joe, Locust Grove, Lone Pine, and Diaz Lake. For RV camping with full hookups, there is Boulder Creek RV Resort. Cell phone reception is possible around the area and a couple of the campgrounds have fishing access.

ROAD CONDITIONS

Some of the roads in the Alabama Hills are paved and some are dirt. Most of the dirt roads are navigable with a 2 wheel drive vehicle under dry conditions, but beware of sand. Extreme caution should be used when conditions are wet. The arches in the Face Rock, Tuttle Creek, and Gunga Din areas, as well as the Whitney Portal Arch, can be reached by paved roads and some minor hiking. The other areas require driving on dirt roads to access.

ORGANIZATION

I have grouped the arches of the Alabama Hills into areas to make them easier to discuss, visit, and locate on a map. By design, you should be able to drive to one of these areas and discover the arches using the associated maps. A GPS capable of expressing latitude and longitude in the form hddd°mm.mmm' will greatly facilitate this endeavor but is not necessary.

SIZE, RATING, NAME

There are two reasons that I have included a description of the size of an arch and a qualitative rating of its' visual appearance. They can help determine if the arch is personally worth searching out and they can help verify the identity of the arch.

In regards to size, these are merely relative estimates and none of the arches were actually measured with any form of ruler. When size is given, it refers to the greatest linear distance in the opening in the arch. So, this may be vertical, horizontal, or diagonal.

The ratings are purely my judgment as to the relative aesthetics of an arch. I take into consideration photographic properties (view), size, accessibility, quality of the rock, and uniqueness. I use a scale of 1 to 5 with 1 being the least appealing and 5 the most. This, then, would be a general description of the rating scale with examples from the Arch Trail Area (ATA) and Face Rock Area (FRA):

Rating	Description	Arch Example
1	Small, difficult to locate, common, nondescript appearance	Movie Road (ATA)
2	Interesting but doesn't really stand out compared to other arches	Little Heart (FRA)
3	Worth seeing, some characteristics of a 5 rating but not all, may be unique	Heart (ATA)
4	Possesses many of the qualities of a 5 but not all	Lathe (ATA)
5	Large, good view, very accessible, very photographic, appealing	Mobius (ATA)

In some cases, I have given an arch a rating with a + sign (for example, 4+). I've done this when I feel an arch is better than most arches with the same number rating but not good enough to go to the next level.

The size and rating of an arch is given with its' GPS coordinate unless it is given in the written text. For example, Mobius Arch would be described like this: (N36 36.813 W118 07.546, R5, 12'). R5 indicates it has a rating of 5, and 12' estimates the size of the opening at twelve feet.

In my text, I mostly focus on arches with a rating of 3 or higher, but I will list data for lesser arches and include their locations on the maps.

For consistency, I tried to use the arch names used by Eugene Carsey and Bob Fagley on their websites. Occasionally, I would come upon an arch that I couldn't find in their collections, so I came up with my own name. When this is the case, I've put an asterisk behind the name (for example, Flower Arch*).

MAPS
The Alabama Hills Area Map gives the relative locations of the different areas discussed in the text. Each area has its own detailed map. All of these maps are to scale, are aligned with north at the top, and display the exact location of the arches.

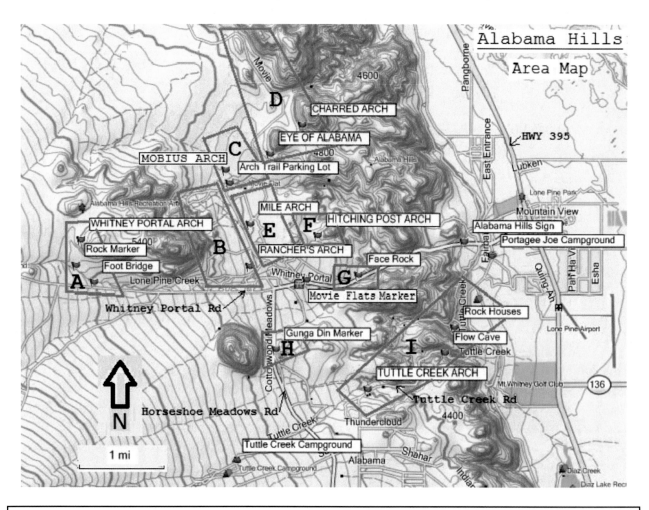

ALABAMA HILLS AREA MAP KEY (includes page where area is discussed in the text):
A-Whitney Portal Arch, p5   D-Eye of Alabama Hills Area, p8   G-Face Rock Area, p24
B-Movie Rd West Area, p11   E-Movie Rd East Area, p13   H-Gunga Din Area, p23
C-Arch Trail Area, p6   F-Beach Area, p17   I-Tuttle Creek Rd Area, p20

SUGGESTED ITINERARIES

In this section, I make some recommendations to help you plan an itinerary for seeing the arches that will fit your schedule. Note, to get the best pictures of the arches, with the Sierras in the background, the ideal lighting occurs in the A.M. hours, but the arches are fun to see at any time of day.

If only a couple of hours are available, then you should concentrate on the "Big Three" and the arches near them. These include Whitney Portal Arch, Mobius Arch, and the Eye of Alabama Arch and they can be seen in that order. To see Mobius Arch, you will need to hike the Arch Trail so you will also get to see Heart Arch and Lathe Arch.

To see all the arches I have included would take approximately three days. One day could start with Whitney Portal Arch, the Face Rock Area, the Tuttle Creek Road Area, and the Gunga Din Area. Another day could consist of the Beach Area and the Movie Road East Area. A third day could be comprised of the Movie Road West Area, the Arch Trail Area, and the Eye of Alabama Area.

WHITNEY PORTAL ARCH   (N36 36.139 W118 09.343, R5, 7')

I consider this arch to be one of the "Big Three" of the Alabama Hills, along with Mobius and the Eye of Alabama, one of the "must sees." It can be viewed from Whitney Portal Road (N36 35.717 W118 09.575), but it really needs to be approached to be appreciated. The opening is approximately seven feet across and I rate it a 5.

To view the arch from the road, go to the GPS coordinate above and look to the northeast. The arch can be seen along the ridgeline. To hike to the arch, go to N36 35.726 W118 09.182. There is a parking area and a footbridge that allows Lone Pine Creek to be crossed. Follow the trail until a rock marker is reached at N36 35.890 W118 09.405. The arch can be seen from here, so head cross-country in that general direction (north). The hike is a relatively easy 1.5 miles roundtrip and takes less than an hour. An aluminum ladder has been left at the arch to get in position to take an interesting picture from the east with Mt. Whitney in the background.

Whitney Portal Arch Map

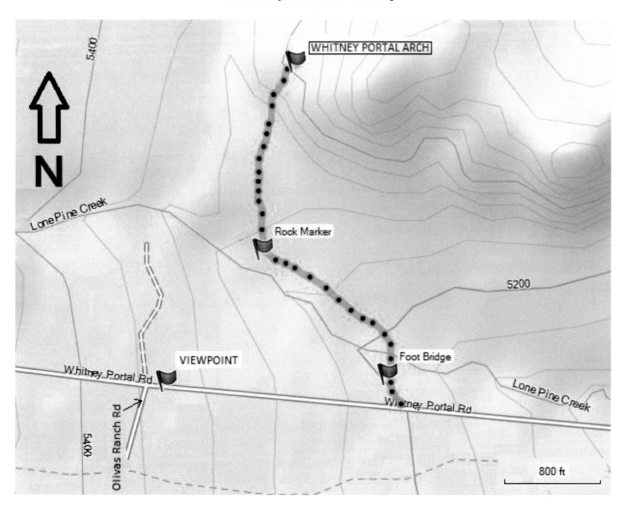

Whitney Portal Arch Pictures

Whitney Portal Arch from the west.   From the east, with Mt. Whitney behind.

ARCH TRAIL AREA

This area gets more foot traffic than any of the other areas and most of that is on the Arch Trail which leads to two spectacular arches, Mobius Arch and Lathe Arch. In addition, Heart Arch can be easily seen.

To reach this area, drive down Movie Road to the Arch Trail parking lot (N36 36.685 W118 07.497). From the parking area, Heart Arch (N36 36.781 W118 07.387, R3, 3') can be seen to the northeast. The clearly marked Arch Trail starts on the west side of the parking area. Follow the trail to Mobius Arch (N36 36.813 W118 07.546, R5, 12'). Just to the west is Lathe Arch (N36 36.802 W118 07.556, R4, 6').

To see the rest of the arches in this area will require some easy cross country hiking from Mobius Arch. I suggest going out to Space Case Arch (N36 37.032 W118 07.442, R3, 5'), first. Baseball Bat Arch (N36 37.034 W118 07.448, R3, 5') is 25 feet to the north of Space Case. From here, head to the southeast to see Sharks Tooth Arch (N36 36.872 W118 07.302, R3, 2.5'). Behind the Heart Arch (N36 36.786 W118 07.373, R3, 4') and Heart Arch (N36 36.781 W118 07.387, R3, 3') can be seen on the way back to the parking lot. Movie Road Arch (N36 36.738 W118 07.112, R1, 5') is best seen as it is passed by while driving on Movie Road.

Arch Trail Area Map

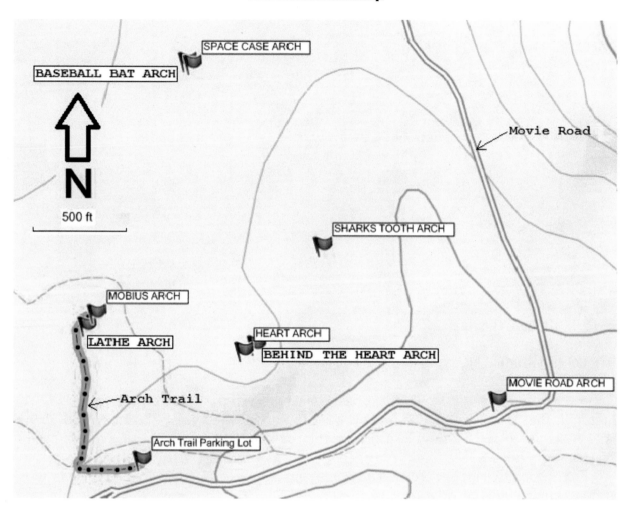

Arch Trail Area Pictures

Mobius Arch   Lathe Arch

Space Case with Baseball Bat right & below

Behind the Heart Arch

Sharks Tooth

Heart Arch

EYE OF ALABAMA AREA

Head north down Movie Road past the Arch Trail parking to reach this area. The first arch that is encountered is one of the "Big Three," the Eye of Alabama (N36 36.969 W118 07.000, R5, 6'). It can be seen from the road and may easily be reached via a short cross country hike.

The next two arches are off a dirt road that connects to Movie Road. Travel to these arches requires hiking or a high clearance vehicle. The first arch you will come to is Charred Arch (N36 37.246 W118 06.604, R4, 22'). It can be seen from the dirt road at N36 37.159 W118 06.668. This arch is the largest at twenty-two feet, even though it is supported in three places. Its' appearance is accented with desert varnish, an orange-yellow to black coating found on rock surfaces in arid environments.

Continuing south on the dirt road will bring you to a small pass and the end of the track. There is a nice view of Owens Lake from here as well as two interesting features. One is Pass Arch* (N36 36.927 W118 06.338, R2, 4') which is at ground level. The other is a good example of exfoliated granite (N36 36.915 W118 06.347). This feature occurs when granitic rock is moved to the surface by tectonic activity and the pressure on the rock that is released causes it to expand slightly. The result is the rock appears to be peeling off in layers like an onion skin.

Returning to Movie Road and traveling north brings you to the next set of arches, Bikini Top Arch (N36 37.800 W118 07.299, R3+, 4') and Stevenson Arch (N36 37.770 W118 07.281, R3, 5'). There is a place to park just off the road to the west and a short hike will be required to see the arches. The first one you will come to is Bikini Top Arch which is appropriately named. For the purpose of scale, each breast is about seven feet in diameter and the tie in the middle is about a foot long. Stevenson Arch is another two hundred feet to the south and about forty feet above ground level.

The last arches in this area are a little further to the north and parking can be located along the edge of Movie Road. These are the Big Daddy Arches (N36 38.136 W118 07.316). Closest to the road is Big Daddy Arch (R2, 8'). This arch reminds me of the Thing in The Fantastic Four. Ten feet to the east is East of Big Daddy Arch (R2, 6'), a much nicer specimen.

Eye of Alabama Area Map

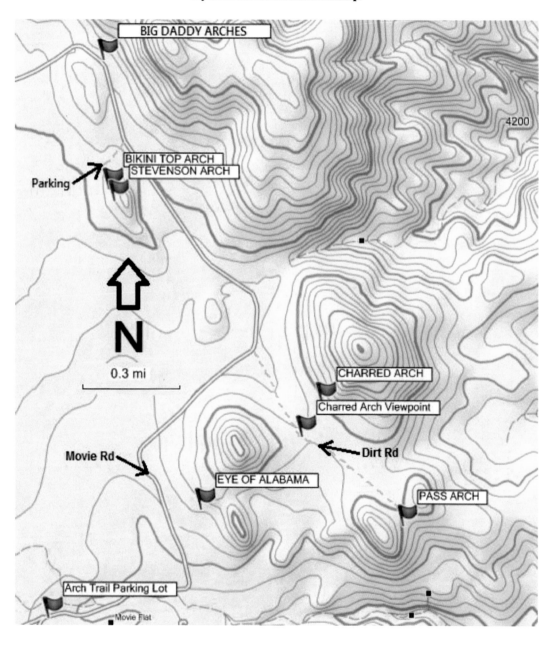

Eye of Alabama

Charred Arch

Pass Arch*

Exfoliated Granite

Bikini Top Arch

Stevenson Arch

Big Daddy Arch

East of Big Daddy Arch

MOVIE ROAD WEST AREA

All of the arches in this area can be approached via dirt roads that are accessible by a 2WD vehicle during dry conditions, but use caution around sand. The map of this section shows some of the key roads and the arches can be located by orienting them with those roads and the surrounding topography as it matches the map's contour lines.

As you enter the Alabama Hills on Movie Road from the south, the first arches will be the Rancher's. Rancher's Arch No. 1 (N36 35.881 W118 07.248, R3, 3' & 1.5') is about one hundred feet from the parking area (N36 35.871 W118 07.227) and can be seen from there. It consists of two holes, one three feet across and the other about one and a half. Another twenty-five feet to the west is Rancher's Arch No. 2 (N36 35.883 W118 07.254, R3, 6').

The next arch traveling north is Ram Head Arch (N36 35.989 W118 07.367, R3, 1.5'). It can be found in a low area at ground level about fifty feet to the south of a parking/camping area.

Further to the north and back up in a small canyon is Rebel Arch (N36 36.144 W118 07.736, R2, 6'). It can be seen from the end of the road and is to the southwest along the ridgeline.

The four remaining arches in this area are clustered together a little farther to the north, and they can all be seen at various places from the road. Graffiti Arch (N36 36.489 W118 07.573, R2, 7') is at ground level but is not in a very aesthetic location. Camp 3 Arch (N36 36.396 W118 07.736, R1+, 8'?) can be seen from the road towards the southeast and near the top of the rock formation. Cave Arch (N36 36.454 W118 07.772, R3, 10') is at ground level near a campsite and it's big enough to enter. Camp 4 arch (N36 36.450 W118 07.934, R2, 8') is also at ground level and is about thirty feet to the west of the parking area. This is also the site of a popular rock climbing face.

Movie Road West Area Map

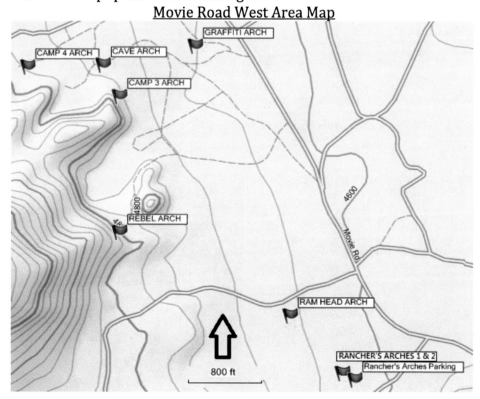

11

Movie Road West Area Pictures

Rancher's Arch No. 1 (from the west)

Rancher's Arch No. 2

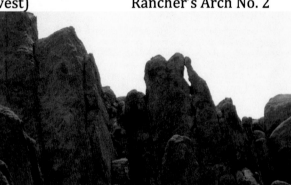

Ram Head Arch

Rebel Arch

Graffiti Arch

Camp 3 Arch (center top of picture)

Cave Arch

Camp 4 Arch

MOVIE ROAD EAST AREA

This area has a good concentration of interesting arches. Some can be seen near the main, 2WD, dirt roads that access the area and others require hiking and/or 4WD. Also, this is a popular area for primitive camping, especially between Old Tom Arch and Grim Arch. I will start my descriptions in the southern region of the area and work north and eventually northeast.

At N36 36.093 W118 06.852 there is a rock foundation that is the remnant of some previous unknown structure. I have no information on its' history, but it is worth viewing.

Old Tom Arch (N36 36.088 W118 07.106, R3, 2') and Brena Arch (N36 36.130 W118 07.080, R3, 7') are easy to locate and view in the southern part of this area. Brena Arch is at ground level in the primitive camping area and Old Tom Arch can be seen in the rocks looking southwest from there.

Traveling north from Brena Arch, the dirt road will make a ninety degree turn to the right. This is a good place to park and hike to Grim Arch (N36 36.255 W118 07.142, R3+, 6'). This arch is at ground level and you can bend over and walk through it. Also, in the parking area, two other minor arches can be seen at ground level. One is Cyclops Arch* (N36 36.234 W118 07.123, R2, 3') and the other is Could-It-Be Arch* (N36 36.222 W118 07.132, R2, 2').

Where the dirt road turns left and north is a 4WD road that continues eastward. Up this road is a minor arch at ground level called Upper Lip Arch* (N36 36.266 W118 06.996, R2+, 4').

Continuing northward on the main dirt road brings you to a 4WD track on the right and within close proximity of Laughing Arch (N36 36.316 W118 07.159, R3 3.5') on the left. The arch can be seen from the road. Taking the 4WD track will bring you to a dead end where there is parking. There are several interesting features to see in this vicinity which I will describe. The road use to continue onward but was closed when a large piece of rock slid off the outcrop to the left and blocked the track in a good example of mass wasting (N36 36.355 W118 07.034). A fun arch to try to locate in the distance from the parking area (N36 36.338 W118 07.061) is Elusive Arch (R2, ?). It is on the skyline to the east on the left side of the tallest peak. To the north are three large rocks that look as if they were neatly set there by a giant (N36 36.362 W118 07.069). A short walk will allow you to see two notable arches, Petroglyth 2 Arch (N36 36.377 W118 07.040, R3, 8') and Slot Canyon Arch* (N36 36.342 W118 07.101, R3, 4'). Slot Canyon Arch is in a 2.5 foot wide slot in the rocks, fifteen feet in from the mouth of the opening, at ground level. It is about two hundred feet to the west of 3 Rocks and is a bit of a challenge to find.

An optional excursion from this point requires some hiking and driving on a 4WD road. The reward is getting to see at least four more arches. Choosing to explore this area will require you to go east at the next fork in the main dirt road. A second right will put you on a 4WD track that crosses a dry ravine. Continuing to the end of the road, you will arrive at a primitive camping area and a place to park. Nearby is Silly (also known as Contortion) Arch (N36 36.310 W118 06.902, R3, 2.5' & 1.5'). It is comprised of two holes on the side of an outcrop and it has a good view of the Sierras in the background. From here, Keith Arch (N36 36.452 W118 06.793, R3, 7' & 4') can be reached via an easy hike across relatively flat terrain. It is a ground level arch with two openings. Two minor arches are passed on the way out to Keith. Reacquire your vehicle and travel northward on the 4WD track as close as you can get to Hole In Thumb Arch* (N36 36.478 W118 06.882, R3, 2.5'). Walk towards the east to find what looks like a mitten with a hole through its' thumb. From the backside, there is a great view of the Sierras through the arch. Walking to the southeast brings you to Wannabe 3 Arch* (N36 36.457 W118 06.871, R2, 2'). This arch sits between two rock formations that could become arches with further erosion.

Going westward will bring you back to Movie Road. Just before you reach it, Mile Arch (N36 36.291 W118 07.244, R3+, 3') can be seen to the south. Supposedly, it was given this name because it is approximately one mile into the Alabama Hills on Movie Road. There is parking near the arch and short hike to the south will bring you to an interesting geologic feature (N36 36.264 W118 07.227). It looks like a rock fence but it is actually a dike that runs through the area from northeast to southwest. A dike is formed when molten rock shoots into cracks in a preexisting rock and then cools and hardens. The result is a vein of rock of notably different chemistry and appearance. In this case, the dike is more resistant to erosion than the surrounding rock so it sticks out vertically and gives the appearance of a fence.

Movie Road East Area Map

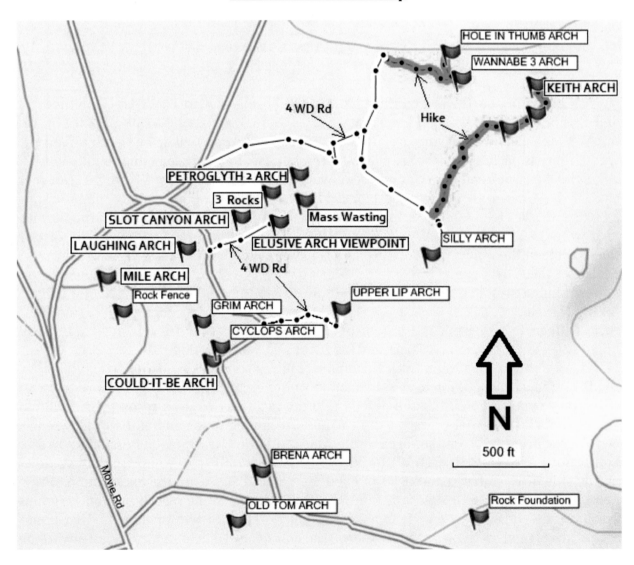

Movie Road East Area Pictures

Rock Foundation

Old Tom Arch

Brena Arch

Grim Arch

Upper Lip Arch*

Laughing Arch

Mass wasting closes road

3 Rocks

Petroglyth 2 Arch

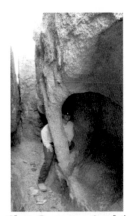

Slot Canyon Arch*

Silly/Contortion Arch

Keith Arch

Hole In Thumb Arch*

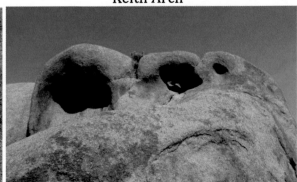

Wannabe 3 Arch*

Mile Arch

Rock Fence

BEACH AREA

Personally, I think this is the most fun area to explore because it has the greatest concentration of arches in the smallest area. In addition, the arches are very unique and few people venture into this part of the Alabama Hills. You may have noticed from the map that many of the arches and features in this area have an ocean related theme. This is why I refer to it as the Beach Area.

To drive into this section definitely requires 4WD because a deep, sandy, dry creek bed needs to be crossed. Accessing the area with 2WD will require parking before the wash and hiking the rest of the way. Otherwise, continue on and park at N36 36.155 W118 06.422. I will describe this collection of arches going in a counterclockwise rotation from this point. To see all of the arches here will require some scrambling on the rocks.

The first arch encountered is Unknown 2 Arch (N36 36.153 W118 06.394 , R4, 4'). If you know where to look, it can be seen from the 4WD track. This arch has an excellent view in the background, and there is a small, 10 inch arch immediately to the west of it called Dolphin Arch (N36 36.153 W118 06.394, R2, 10") that can be seen, as well.

The next arch is Surfer No. 3 (N36 36.172 W118 06.433, R3+, 4'). It is another arch that has a respectable view through it and it can also be seen from the 4WD track.

One of the standout arches in this area is the Hitching Post (N36 36.182 W118 06.411, R4, 12'). It is at ground level and unfortunately there isn't a good associated view, but its' appearance and size make it unique.

The next two arches and one rock formation continue the ocean theme. First, is Surfer No. 2 Arch (N36 36.191 W118 06.409, R3, 3'). It is about forty feet north of the Hitching Post. A short distance to the west is the Whale's Head*/Wave (N36 36.190 W118 06.420). It's not an arch but it is an interesting structure none the less. Just a little further west and a little north is Surfer No. 1 Arch (N36 36.197 W118 06.436, R3, 4'). This is the least aesthetic of the Surfers, and the hardest to find, even though it is possible to see from the 4WD track. With a little rock climbing, a view of the Sierras can be lined up through the arch.

Three minor arches can be seen on the way to Craggy Arch. These are Stab Arch (N36 36.212 W118 06.379, R1, 2'), Side Rock Arch* (N36 36.239 W118 06.423, R1+, 14"), and Eyebrow Arch* (N36 36.242 W118 06.440, R2, 3'& 3'). I only mention these because they are fun and quick to find. Craggy Arch (N36 36.272 W118 06.523, R3, 4', 3', & 2') is comprised of a cluster of three arches found at ground level and is the northernmost arch in this area.

The remainder of the arches are all on the west side of the 4WD track and can be divided into minor arches in the north and better arches to the south. There are four minor arches which I will describe from north to south. I include these because they are fun to locate. The first is Bird Eye (N36 36.223 W118 06.707, R2, 3' & 8'). It can be seen from the road and is composed of a larger arch below a smaller one. Next up is Afternoon Arch* (N36 36.196 W118 06.634, R1, 8"). Sun rays pass nicely through this arch in the afternoon and it can be seen from Craggy Arch. Continuing eastward is Baby Arch (N36 36.190 W118 06.597, R1, 2.5'). It is hidden behind and to the west of a large slab of rock. To the south and east is the last minor arch, Sandwich Arch (N36 36.165 W118 06.578, R2+, 2'). To appreciate this one, and the view through it, it needs to be observed from its' west side.

The last features to see in this area can all be found within approximately 300 feet of each other. As a matter of fact, two of the remaining three arches can be seen from Mushroom Rock* (N36 36.154 W118 06.538), so we will start there. Mushroom Rock is possible to see from Sandwich Arch and is a little to the south and east of that feature. From Mushroom Rock, towards the south, Domino Arch (N36 36.126 W118 06.528, R3, 2.5') is visible. Actually, this arch can be seen from all around the Beach Area. The best lighting for photographing this arch occurs in the morning hours. Concluding the beach theme is Lifeguard Arch (N36 36.161 W118 06.508, R3, 6') which can be seen to the north and east of Mushroom Rock. This arch can also be seen from numerous locations around the area. Down in the rocks and ravines between Domino and Lifeguard are the Fraternal Twins Arches* (N36 36.140 W118 06.517, R3, 7'). Within eight feet of each other are two similar arches that make up the Twins. A cluster of small, nameless arches are in the vicinity.

<u>Beach Area Map</u>

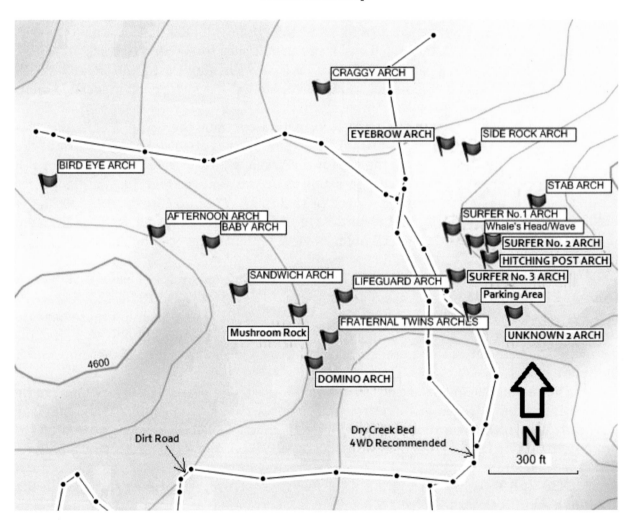

Beach Area Pictures

Unknown 2 Arch

Surfer No. 3 Arch

Hitching Post Arch

Surfer No. 2 Arch

Whale's Head*/Wave

Surfer No. 1 Arch

Craggy Arch

Sandwich Arch

Mushroom Rock*   Domino Arch

Lifeguard Arch   One of the Fraternal Twins*

TUTTLE CREEK ROAD AREA

This collection of arches can be reached via paved roads with a 2WD vehicle and minimal hiking. To access this area, turn onto Tuttle Creek Road from Whitney Portal Road and head south.

Upon crossing a bridge, you will come to a dirt road called Indian Cemetery Road. An interesting side trip is to take this dirt road to the northwest which will bring you to two rock houses (N36 35.294 W118 04.731) that were apparently used to store explosives. Continuing down the road and going right at the intersection will bring you to the Indian Cemetery (not shown on the map). It is in the mouth of a canyon to the west (N36 35.699 W118 04.693).

The next stop, after returning to the paved road and continuing south and then west, is the flow cave/miner's dugout (N36 35.044 W118 04.846). This feature can be seen from the road and there is a wide area there for parking.

The road continues up Tuttle Canyon and eventually crosses Tuttle Creek in a dip in the road. From this point, Tuttle Canyon Arch is visible from the road towards the south along the ridgeline (N36 34.880 W118 05.133, R3, 8'?). A little farther down the road is the viewpoint for seeing Fish Arch and Duck Arch (N36 34.819 W118 05.157, R3, 4-6'?). They are on the north side of the road, approximately twenty feet below the skyline, and the Fish is on the left and the Duck is on the right. You can make out the Fish's eye (the arch), head, and scales and it appears to be on the Duck's back. The Duck is represented as a head with a beak which is to the right of the eye (the arch).

Further up the canyon is a dirt pullout on the north side of the road. Park here. A short walk to the north, approximately fifty feet, brings you to a green gate. Nearby is a small arch, Green Gate Arch* (N36 34.688 W118 05.792, R2, 1'). Go through the gate and you will find Tuttle Creek Arch which spans the creek (N36 34.697 W118 05.794, R4, 20').

As you continue up the canyon, the paved road will make a half circle around a large granite outcrop. There is a dirt cutoff for this half circle, but it is quite sandy and requires 4WD. Taking the dirt road from either end allows you to drive up to the last two arches. The other alternative is to park where the dirt road meets the end of the half circle and then walk (N36 34.406 W118 05.895).

Tuttle Creek Road Arch (N36 34.490 W118 05.948, R2, 3') can be seen from the paved road near the end of the half circle. In the same area are at least 4 more smaller arches. In addition, an interesting geological feature nearby is a cave in a boulder that could easily provide shelter for two people during inclement weather (N36 34.477 W118 05.934).

To the east a short distance is an intriguing arch that looks like the electrode end of a spark plug. Fittingly, it is named Spark Plug Arch (N36 34.449 W118 05.697, R3, 5'?).

This completes the Tuttle Creek Road Area. Continuing south on Tuttle Creek Road will bring you to Sunset Drive. Making a right here will bring you to Horseshoe Meadows Road. Taking this road north will bring you back to Whitney Portal Road.

<u>Tuttle Creek Road Area Map</u>

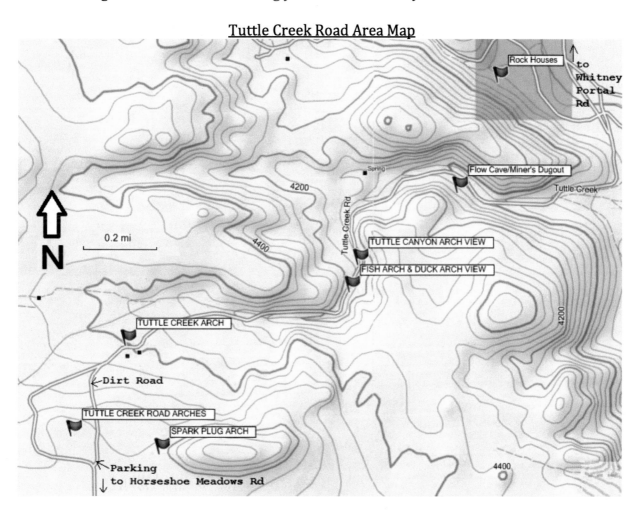

Tuttle Creek Road Area Pictures

Rock House

Flow Cave

Tuttle Canyon Arch

Fish and Duck Arches

Tuttle Creek Arch

Tuttle Creek Road Arch

Boulder Cave

Spark Plug Arch

GUNGA DIN AREA

This area provides access to a couple of interesting arches as well as an historical plaque. Go to the Gunga Din Marker located at N36 35.078 W118 06.927. There is abundant parking in the area and all of the arches can be reached within short walking distance. In the picture of the marker below, the left side of the marker lines up with the location of Eagle's Head Arch (N36 35.072 W118 06.894, R3, 2') and the right side lines up with Gunga Din Arch (N36 35.067 W118 06.887, R3, 4'). Across Horseshoe Meadows Road, from the marker, West Gunga Din/Palette Arch (N36 35.046 W118 06.999, R3, 2.5') can be seen. It is at ground level.

To see some other arches in the area, start at the marker and walk down the dirt road towards the east. Hell's Gate Arch (N36 35.085 W118 06.848, R2, 6') will be along the road on the right. Rabbit Arch (R2+, 4') is located immediately behind Hell's Gate Arch. Across the road is Rock Top Arch* (N36 35.089 W118 06.846, R1, 8"). For a good GPS challenge, try to locate Flower Arch* (N36 35.032 W118 06.949, R1, 5"), a circular rock with a hole near the center.

Gunga Din Area Map

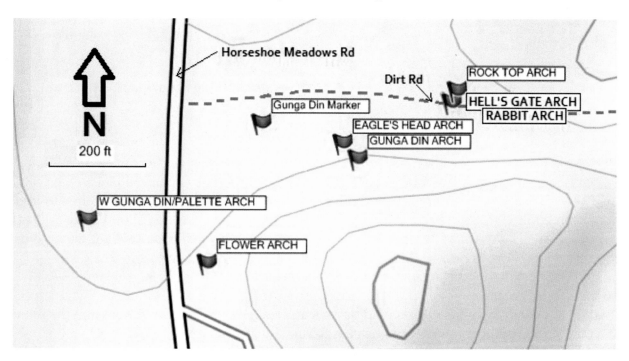

Gunga Din Area Pictures

Gunga Din Marker

Eagle's Head Arch

Gunga Din Arch

West Gunga Din/Palette Arch

FACE ROCK AREA

This is an easy area to reach with paved road access. As you head west on Whitney Portal Road, you will notice a large rock on the north side that is painted like a face (N36 35.797 W118 05.909). There is a parking area near the face and the three arches in this area can be hiked to from here. Although there is nothing spectacular about these arches, they are usually the first ones people see and I've observed that kids really have a good time searching for and finding them. They can all be walked right up to and touched.

The first arch to be encountered is Little Heart Arch (N36 35.792 W118 05.973, R2, 18") and it is composed of two arches together. Farther west at ground level is an arch that, from the south, looks like it could have been created by a large bullet passing through the rock. Not finding a name for it, I called it Shot Rock Arch* (N36 35.754 W118 06.061, R2, 1'). A little farther to the west is West of Face Rock Arch (N36 35.724 W118 06.067, R2+, 3').

Driving a little further down Whitney Portal Road, you will find the Movie Flats Marker (N36 35.749 W118 06.548). It commemorates all the movies that have been filmed in the area and locates the beginning of Movie Road.

Face Rock Area Map

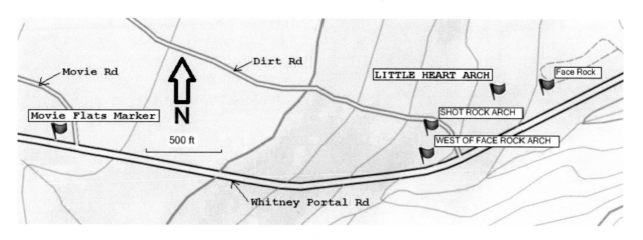

Face Rock Area Pictures

Face Rock

Little Heart Arch

Shot Rock Arch*

West of Face Rock Arch

Movie Flats Marker

EPILOGUE

This concludes my guide to the arches of the Alabama Hills. I hope that you have found it an informative, educational, and beneficial resource as you have explored the region. If it has wet your appetite to discover more arches, there is an area in the Alabama Hills further to the north and east that I did not cover in my guidebook. It contains arches with names like Astronomer, Hammerhead, and North Sentry. If you feel inclined to seek out those rock structures, then I bid you farewell and happy arch hunting!

ABOUT THE AUTHOR

Orlyn Fordham was born in Kalispell, Montana in 1954. He has lived in Washington and California and he currently resides in Nevada. He earned a Bachelor's degree in Earth Science from California State University, Northridge and a teaching credential in Physical Science from California State University, Fullerton. After 27 years of teaching in public schools, Orlyn retired.

Besides viewing arches, the author enjoys riding motorcycles, traveling, hunting, fishing, camping, freestyle Frisbee, snowboarding, rafting, mountain biking, surfing, wakeboarding, playing guitar and harmonica, and flying RC planes.

APPENDIX

DATA BY AREA

NAME OF ARCH OR FEATURE	LATITUDE-LONGITUDE	SIZE	RATING
WHITNEY PORTAL ARCH (P) (page 5)	N36 36.139 W118 09.343	7'	5
Foot Bridge	N36 35.726 W118 09.182		
Rock Marker	N36 35.890 W118 09.405		
WPA VIEWPOINT - ROAD	N36 35.717 W118 09.575		
EYE OF ALABAMA AREA (page 8)			
Exfoliated Granite (P)	N36 36.915 W118 06.347		
Charred Arch Viewpoint	N36 37.159 W118 06.668		
BIG DADDY ARCH (P)	N36 38.136 W118 07.316	8'	2
BIKINI TOP ARCH (P)	N36 37.800 W118 07.299	4'	3+
CHARRED ARCH (P)	N36 37.246 W118 06.604	22'	4
EAST OF BIG DADDY ARCH (P)	N36 38.136 W118 07.316	6'	2
EYE OF ALABAMA (P)	N36 36.969 W118 07.000	6'	5
PASS ARCH* (P)	N36 36.927 W118 06.338	4'	2
STEVENSON ARCH (P)	N36 37.770 W118 07.281	5'	3
ARCH TRAIL AREA (page 6)			
Arch Trail Parking Lot	N36 36.685 W118 07.497		
BASEBALL BAT ARCH (P)	N36 37.034 W118 07.448	5'	3
BEHIND THE HEART ARCH (P)	N36 36.786 W118 07.373	4'	3
HEART ARCH (P)	N36 36.781 W118 07.387	3'	3
LATHE ARCH (P)	N36 36.802 W118 07.556	6'	4
MOBIUS ARCH (P)	N36 36.813 W118 07.546	12'	5
MOVIE ROAD ARCH	N36 36.738 W118 07.112	5'	1
SHARKS TOOTH ARCH (P)	N36 36.872 W118 07.302	2.5'	3
SPACE CASE ARCH (P)	N36 37.032 W118 07.442	5'	3
FACE ROCK AREA (page 24)			
Face Rock (P)	N36 35.797 W118 05.909		
LITTLE HEART ARCH (P)	N36 35.792 W118 05.973	18"	2
SHOT ROCK ARCH* (P)	N36 35.754 W118 06.061	1'	2
WEST OF FACE ROCK ARCH (P)	N36 35.724 W118 06.067	3'	2+

*Indicates an arch named by the author
(P) Indicates picture is in the text

NAME OF ARCH OR FEATURE	LATITUDE-LONGITUDE	SIZE	RATING
TUTTLE CREEK ROAD AREA (page 20)			
Boulder Cave (P)	N36 34.477 W118 05.934		
Flow Cave (P)	N36 35.044 W118 04.846		
Indian Cemetery	N36 35.699 W118 04.693		
Rock Houses (P)	N36 35.294 W118 04.731		
Tuttle Creek Rd Arch Parking 2WD	N36 34.406 W118 05.895		
FISH ARCH & DUCK ARCH (P)	N36 34.819 W118 05.157	4-6'?	3
GREEN GATE ARCH	N36 34.688 W118 05.792	1'	2
SPARK PLUG ARCH (P)	N36 34.449 W118 05.697	5'?	3
TUTTLE CANYON ARCH VIEW (P)	N36 34.880 W118 05.133	8'?	3
TUTTLE CREEK ARCH (P)	N36 34.697 W118 05.794	20'	4
TUTTLE CREEK ROAD ARCHES (P)	N36 34.490 W118 05.948	3'	2
BEACH AREA (page 17)			
Beach Area Parking	N36 36.155 W118 06.422		
Mushroom Rock (P)	N36 36.154 W118 06.538		
Whale's Head/Wave (P)	N36 36.190 W118 06.420		
AFTERNOON ARCH*	N36 36.196 W118 06.634	8"	1
BABY ARCH	N36 36.190 W118 06.597	2.5'	1
BIRD EYE ARCH	N36 36.223 W118 06.707	3',8'	2
CRAGGY ARCH (P)	N36 36.272 W118 06.523	4',3',2'	3
DOLPHIN ARCH	N36 36.153 W118 06.394	10"	2
DOMINO ARCH (P)	N36 36.126 W118 06.528	2.5'	3
EYE BROW ARCH*	N36 36.242 W118 06.440	3',3'	2
FRATERNAL TWINS ARCHES* (P)	N36 36.140 W118 06.517	7'	3
HITCHING POST ARCH (P)	N36 36.182 W118 06.411	12'	4
LIFEGUARD ARCH (P)	N36 36.161 W118 06.508	6'	3
SANDWICH ARCH (P)	N36 36.165 W118 06.578	2'	2+
SIDE ROCK ARCH*	N36 36.239 W118 06.423	14"	1+
STAB ARCH	N36 36.212 W118 06.379	2'	1
SURFER No.1 ARCH (P)	N36 36.197 W118 06.436	4'	3
SURFER No.2 ARCH (P)	N36 36.191 W118 06.409	3'	3
SURFER No.3 ARCH (P)	N36 36.172 W118 06.433	4'	3+
UNKNOWN 2 ARCH (P)	N36 36.153 W118 06.394	4'	4
GUNGA DIN AREA (page 23)			
Gunga Din Marker (P)	N36 35.078 W118 06.927		
EAGLE'S HEAD ARCH (P)	N36 35.072 W118 06.894	2'	3
FLOWER ARCH*	N36 35.032 W118 06.949	5"	1
GUNGA DIN ARCH (P)	N36 35.067 W118 06.887	4'	3
HELL'S GATE ARCH	N36 35.085 W118 06.848	6'	2
RABBIT ARCH	N36 35.085 W118 06.848	4'	2+
ROCK TOP ARCH*	N36 35.089 W118 06.846	8"	1
W GUNGA DIN/PALETTE ARCH (P)	N36 35.046 W118 06.999	2.5'	3

*Indicates an arch named by the author
(P) Indicates picture is in the text

NAME OF ARCH OR FEATURE	LATITUDE-LONGITUDE	SIZE	RATING
MOVIE ROAD EAST AREA (page 13)			
3 Rocks (P)	N36 36.362 W118 07.069		
Mass Wasting (P)	N36 36.355 W118 07.034		
Rock Fence (P)	N36 36.264 W118 07.227		
Rock Foundation (P)	N36 36.093 W118 06.852		
BRENA ARCH (P)	N36 36.130 W118 07.080	7'	3
COULD-IT-BE ARCH*	N36 36.222 W118 07.132	2'	2
CYCLOPS ARCH*	N36 36.234 W118 07.123	3'	2
ELUSIVE ARCH VIEWPOINT	N36 36.338 W118 07.061	?	2
GRIM ARCH (P)	N36 36.255 W118 07.142	6'	3+
HOLE IN THUMB ARCH* (P)	N36 36.478 W118 06.882	2.5'	3
KEITH ARCH (P)	N36 36.452 W118 06.793	7',4'	3
LAUGHING ARCH (P)	N36 36.316 W118 07.159	3.5'	3
MILE ARCH (P)	N36 36.291 W118 07.244	3'	3+
OLD TOM ARCH (P)	N36 36.088 W118 07.106	2'	3
PETROGLYTH 2 ARCH (P)	N36 36.377 W118 07.040	8'	3
SILLY ARCH (P)	N36 36.310 W118 06.902	1.5,2.5	3
SLOT CANYON ARCH (P)	N36 36.342 W118 07.101	4'	3
UPPER LIP ARCH* (P)	N36 36.266 W118 06.996	4'	2+
WANNABE 3 ARCH* (P)	N36 36.457 W118 06.871	2'	2
MOVIE ROAD WEST AREA (page 11)			
Rancher's Arches Parking	N36 35.871 W118 07.227		
CAMP 3 ARCH (P)	N36 36.396 W118 07.736	8'?	1+
CAMP 4 ARCH (P)	N36 36.450 W118 07.934	8'	2
CAVE ARCH (P)	N36 36.454 W118 07.772	10',2'	3
GRAFFITI ARCH (P)	N36 36.489 W118 07.573	7'	2
RAM HEAD ARCH (P)	N36 35.989 W118 07.367	1.5'	3
RANCHER'S ARCH (P)	N36 35.881 W118 07.248	3',1.5'	3
RANCHER'S ARCH NO.2 (P)	N36 35.883 W118 07.254	6'	3
REBEL ARCH (P)	N36 36.144 W118 07.736	6'	2
MISCELLANEOUS WAYPOINTS			
Alabama Hills Sign (P)	N36 36.121 W118 04.613		
Movie Flats Marker (P)	N36 35.749 W118 06.548		
Portagee Joe Campground	N36 35.984 W118 04.278		
Tuttle Creek Campground	N36 34.026 W118 07.410		

*Indicates an arch named by the author
(P) Indicates picture is in the text

Made in United States
Orlando, FL
13 March 2024